TALES FROM THE MINES
BY
GEOFFREY CARR

Sketches by John Creber

a J.N.M. Publication

1986

a J.N.M. Publication

J.N.M. PUBLICATIONS,
WINSTER,
MATLOCK,
DERBYSHIRE,
DE4 2DQ.

Edited, typeset and designed by John N. Merrill.

© Text: Geoffrey Carr

© Sketches: John Creber and J.N.M. Publications.

First published October 1986.

ISBN 0 907496 45 8

Typesetting interfaced by:
Steve Rothwell Typesetting Services, 20 St. Ann's Square, Manchester M2 7HG.

Printed by: Adams & Sons Ltd., Burcott Road, Hereford HR4 9LW.

Contents

About The Author

Geoffrey Carr was born in a tiny cottage in Ossett in 1928 and was educated at local schools, Wakefield Technical College and Thornes House Grammar School, Wakefield.

He entered the mining industry in 1945, starting work in the fitting shop at Old Roundwood Colliery, Ossett, and eventually working underground at this colliery and later at Hartley Bank Colliery, Horbury, where he was employed as a shotfirer and later as a district deputy.

In 1954 he passed the Colliery Manager's examination and decided to leave the industry and enter the teaching profession. A teacher training course at Bolton Technical Teacher Training College provided him with a Certificate of Education, and at the end of the course he was appointed to the post of Assistant Lecturer in the Mining Department at Wakefield Technical College.

Three years later he moved to a post at Whitwood Mining and Technical College, Castleford, where he eventually became a Senior Lecturer in the Mining Department. He retired from the teaching profession in 1984, and now spends his time watching birds, a life-long hobby, writing and helping to care for the St. John's Methodist Church in Ossett, where he is Senior Steward and Property Committee Secretary.

In 1970 he became interested in long-distance walking and helped to form a walking club attached to his Church and of which he is also Secretary. He has organised sponsored walks for many different charities since then, and has personally completed seventeen crossings of the Lyke Wake Walk, being elected to the Melancholly Court of Past Masters of the Lyke Wake Club at their Silver Jubilee in 1980.

In 1978 he devised his own long distance challenge walk, The Cal-Der-Went Walk, a thirty miles walk from the Calder Valley in Yorkshire to the Derwent Valley in Derbyshire, and in 1979 he wrote a guide book for the walk which was published by the Dalesman Publishing Company.

He married his wife Marian, a miner's daughter, in 1951, and still lives at 'Fern Cottage', where the large garden ensures that any spare time will be usefully employed.

Author's Preface

MANY books have been written on mining lore, some of them recording the many disasters that are associated with the industry, while others have concentrated upon the struggle of the miner against the oppressive Coal Owners of the past. In the book, 'Lays and Tales of the Mines', the author outlines some of the horrific happenings in the older mines, the conditions of which would, rightly, not be tolerated today.

In most of these stories, the natural humour of the miner is missing, for the old days were certainly not good ones in the mines and maybe there was very little to laugh about as life was taken much more seriously.

Not all the stories related in this volume pretend to end on a happy note. Mining is not like that, for every year some families are left without the breadwinner because of a fatal accident at one of our mines. Happily though, fatal accidents are far fewer than in the past and major disasters are largely unknown. This is not intended to invoke a complacent attitude, for all persons who are connected with the industry should strive for as safe an environment as is possible in which men can work.

The stories related are collected from personal experiences and from fellow workers and colleagues in many parts of the British coalfield.

Although the incidents related are factual, the names of the collieries and the people involved have been changed.

A glossary of mining terms used in this book is provided at the back of the book. The author wishes to thank Malcolm Blythe for reading the draft of this book and for his helpful criticisms.

Geoffrey Carr 1986

CHAPTER 1

Stuffed Rabbit

'DID I ever tell you about calling for a pint at our local pub?' said Albert one snap time.

He and his mate Len had been working together for many years, and as they had grown older they had been given a roving commission, going into various parts of the mine where roof supports were in need of replacement, or where small roof falls had to be cleared and the mine made safe for working in and travelling through.

Albert and Len had, in their younger days, earned the names of 'Wangem' and 'Bangem' from the time when they were employed in ripping a tail gate and packing the dirt into the waste. It was related that Albert would say, 'You wangem to me and I'll bangem into t' pack'. The names had stuck, as they usually do in such cases, and were used behind their backs and out of earshot.

Len shook his head, a mouthful of fat and bread preventing any useful contribution to the conversation. He knew that Albert would tell his tale anyway. 'Well', continued Albert, having waited long enough for an answer, 'I thought I would just nip in for a quick half on my way from t' pit. I wer spitting feathers. I got half a bitter and nodded the time of day to a young chap at the other end of the bar, when into t' pub came that big chap from Uppertown, what's his name, oh aye, that's it, Jake Todd.' Anyway, Jake asked the young chap if he were having a pint, and he nodded and smiled his thanks. Jake then asked me, 'Are you having a pint?' he said.

'No', I said, 'I'm on my way home and I just popped in for a half to slake my thirst.'.

'You're having a pint or you're having a fight', he said.

'I'm having a pint', I said.

'I got a fight on my hands when I got home though, my dinner was spoiled and it wasn't fit for our dog. My missis wer mad. Well you know our lass, Len, she's a bit slow on the uptake at the best of times, and she couldn't see my side of the story at all.' Len concluded glumly.

'Aye, he's a big chap is Jake Todd', said Len, 'Do you know, Albert, he was the only bloke that I've seen eat a pork pie sandwich', he added.

Albert was all ears.

Len continued his tale: 'He sat down one snap time and pulled this pie out of his tin and put it between two slices of bread.'

Albert had stopped eating his own snap and was watching Len intently.

'He opened his mouth', said Len, 'I shouted at him 'You'll break your jaw', but it was no use, he took one bite and half the pie disappeared into his mouth.'

Albert's jaw had dropped open as he listed to Len's vivid description of the disappearing pork pie, and he was prevented from further eating as his mate continued the story.

'That's not all', Len said. 'When he'd finished the pie, he brought out an apple pie, one of those big ones, about eight or nine inches across. Well, he took one bite out of it, about the size of a saucer. Honest, Albert, there was crumbs falling in his ears.'

'I was rabbit catching last Saturday', said Len, changing the subject. 'I went up on to the common', he added, having finally completed his snap. 'There's plenty of brambles up there and plenty of rabbits as well.'

The common was one of the local beauty spots where blackberries could be collected in season and, also, rabbits abounded. Len was a master at setting snares.

'I went up after tea on Saturday and set half a dozen snares', he recounted. 'And then on Sunday morning, before breakfast, I went back. There was a rabbit in three of them, so that was a good effort.'

2

'How does your missis cook rabbits?' enquired Albert.

'Well', said Len, 'We have them roasted and stewed, but the nicest of all I've tasted was a stuffed one.'

'Stuffed rabbit!', Albert repeated unbelievingly, 'I've never heard of stuffed rabbit.'

'Look', said Len, 'I'll bring you one up to your house this evening and you can try it out for yourself.'

As good as his word, Len delivered the rabbit to Albert's that evening, and then they went off together for a jar or two in the local.

Next day they were back at their work and, during a brief rest, Albert asked, 'What does your missis stuff rabbits with?'.

'Well', replied Len, 'You know rabbits, they like anything green.'

'Anything green', repeated Albert, 'I'll tell her what you said'.

Nothing more was said on the subject until about two days later, when Len casually asked as to whether Albert had enjoyed his rabbit.

'Enjoyed it!', exclaimed Albert, 'We couldn't enjoy that, we couldn't eat the thing.'

'Well', said Len, 'Didn't she stuff it like I said? It should have been alright.'

'She stuffed it alright', said Albert, 'but we couldn't eat it.'

'That's funny', said Len, 'My missis makes lovely stuffed rabbit. Didn't you tell her to stuff it with something green?'

'That was the trouble', said Albert, 'The only thing that she could find that was green was my old green jumper. I tell you, we couldn't eat it. We had to chuck it away!'

CHAPTER 2

The Strange Story of David Banks

GHOST stories and tales of strange sightings are legion amongst the mining communities, some being handed down through the generations of mining men, embroidered in the passage of time, and no doubt some of them are entirely invention. Classic examples include the story told of a disappearing miner who had been spoken to as he passed a lone compressor attendant, and, according to the teller of the tale, just vanished from sight. Or of the two colliery officials who saw a man enter a part of a mine where no one else was present. When they examined that part of the pit, they could not find any sight or sound of the man.

Fred Bowers had collapsed and died as he worked with his mates, at the face of a stone drift at one mine. On the next night shift following the accident, the deputy in charge was about to start an inspection of the tunnel, leaving the workmen at the entrance to the workings.

Suddenly the signal bell for the drift conveyor rang once! The deputy went white. Who had rung that bell? Nobody was supposed to be up there. Nobody was up there, and yet the signal bell had rung and everyone waiting at the entrance to the drift had heard it.

One of the workmen said, 'It's old Bowers come back to haunt you!' The men had a good laugh, the deputy only half-heartedly joining in, for he was the one who had to go up that drift, alone, to make his inspection.

In the light of day it is easy to offer explanations for weird events, but in the dark depths of a mine, when one is about to go into a part of a mine where no-one is supposed to be, it is enough to turn a strong man's legs to jelly. One such event is related in the story of David Banks.

Banks had been a deputy at Bellshaw Colliery for about eighteen years, and in his time he had been responsible for many successful coal faces. He was considered reliable, sober and unflappable. He was in the fortunate position of being regarded as a good deputy by both senior management and the workmen. Bellshaw Pit had been worked out and had closed down, and David Banks had moved to the nearby Boulty Pit. What it was that turned this solid, dependable man into a gibbering, shaking mass of human flesh in the April of that year, took a long time in telling, and it was many months later when the full story emerged.

It was Banks' first shift at Boulty Pit as deputy in charge of 300's unit. It was a night shift.

The seam being worked was about a yard thick, and there had been some geological problems associated with faulty ground near the return end of the face line, which often held up coal production while the cutter-loader sheared through the broken rocks.

About three months earlier, a bad fall in this area had pinned Frank Ames to the conveyor, suffocating him before willing hands had secured the roof and pulled the fallen rocks away from his body.

On the night in question, coal production had stopped on Banks' district. That fact was an easy one to deduce, for there was no coal coming off the gate conveyor belt. The deputy walked down the main gate of his unit to investigate the cause, only to find that the trouble was in the usual spot, two hundred and fifty yards away at the other end of the face line. There was nothing else for it but to scramble back along the face line for the second time within the hour. David Banks was far from pleased.

Leaving word with the conveyor attendant as to where he was going, he started along the face. Somewhere in the middle of the face line, about one hundred yards from the far end of the unit, the spot light on Banks' helmet picked out the figure of a man squatting comfortably on one knee in the travelling track of the chocks.

The man didn't seem inclined to move, and the deputy's temper wasn't improved when he failed to get any response as to who he was or if it was he who had stopped the face conveyor. There was a signal unit on the spillplate assembly at the side of the conveyor, and Banks could see that it was from this very point that the conveyor had in fact been stopped. The deputy operated the signal and restarted the conveyor, waiting a few minutes until the coal was flowing along the conveyor again, and then he clambered around the man and continued on the face and into the tailgate.

Three rippers were working in the return gate, and when the deputy arrived there he stopped a while for a chat.

Banks then remembered the man in the chocks down the face line and realised that he had assumed that he was a member of the cutter-loader team, but that team was fully manned. He wasn't a member of the ripping team either, for it was normal policy for three men to rip the return gates at Boulty Pit. The deputy asked the rippers if they had seen anything of the man earlier in the shift—had he come past them onto the face?

They shook their heads. No-one had come down the return gate since the supply lads had delivered the last lot of supports earlier in the shift, and they had gone back up the gate again about an hour previously.

'What did this man look like?' asked the chargeman.

Banks realised after a moment's thought that he didn't know what he looked like. 'He was just a bloke like you or me. He had knee pads, dark trousers, football jersey, aye, red and white stripes', he said, adding, 'I can't think of anything else about him.'

'Frank Ames used to wear a red and white jersey, didn't he?', one of the rippers interjected.

'Who is Frank Ames?', queried Banks.

The chargeman then related how Ames had been killed on that face by a fall of roof, some months previously.

David Banks went weak at the knees. He knew then who, or rather what, he had seen crouched in the chocks only moments before, just back along the face line, and nothing in the world would make him go back.

He could hardly speak when the rippers asked him if anything was wrong. He staggered up the gate, glassy-eyed and muttering incomprehensibly.

Banks never stopped until he reached the pit bottom, and there he could not explain his predicament to the undermanager who escorted him out of the mine. David Banks was off work for a couple of months, eventually asking for a surface job.

He never went below ground again.

CHAPTER 3

The Phantom Strikes

TO EAT another man's snap, or to drink from his water bottle without first asking his permission, is one of the worst crimes one miner may commit against his fellows.

The supplies lads on 5—Wests unit at Old Bankwood Colliery were in no doubt that someone was pilfering the water supplies from their water bottles. They always left their snap and water bottles at the gate end while they made a delivery of arch girders and other supports down to the coal face and, on almost every shift, one or other of them reported that some water had been drunk, and some bottles were left quite empty.

The phantom had struck again!

Who could the phantom be? Suspects were listed mentally, and some were discounted on the grounds that they just would not do such a thing.

As the drinking water kept disappearing, it was obvious to the lads that some action was needed in order to find the culprit, and a plan of action was devised.

One bottle of water was to be specially prepared—not with anything dangerous or nasty, but 'spiked' with something that would make the culprit obvious.

Next day the special bottle was produced and was left in a conspicuous position. Half the shift went by, and the first load of supplies had been delivered to the coal face. The lads had returned to the end of the gate to eat their snap and, to no-one's surprise and everyone's delight, it could be seen that 'the' bottle was empty.

'All we have to do now', said one of the lads, 'is to wait until tomorrow and then we shall know who the thief is.'

'Why, what did you put in it?' asked another.

'Only a good dose of Epsom salts!' said the first.

The deputy, Sam Brett, was away from work for a week. His sick note from the Doctor said, 'gastric', followed by an undecipherable scrawl.

The phantom never manifested itself again on 5—West's face, or anywhere else for that matter. The lesson had been well and truly learned.

CHAPTER 4

'Haircut Sir'

SHORT back and sides was once the standard order of the day when one entered the doorway 'under the barber's pole'. Clippers and scissors, deftly manipulated, swiftly reduced long flowing locks to a mere bristle, perhaps just leaving a few strands, though drastically reduced in length, at the forelock. Such a trim would last seven or eight weeks before a return visit was needed and, further, the hair was easily washed clean after a shift in the dust of a coal mine and it was very good value for money.

Sid's emporium was no exception, although his operation was carried out in the kitchen of his terrace house in the village of Middletown. In warmer weather, his customers would sit on the garden seat outside.

Sid's gatherings were usually on Saturday afternoons, due to his six-day-a-week job at the local pit, where he was in charge of operating a belt conveyor at a transfer point, where the coal was fed onto the trunk conveyor. The job was far from arduous, and the wage that he received was augmented by his Saturday side-line.

There was, however, one hair style and one only. It was 'all off'. On one occasion, a young man came to Sid's with long and flowing locks and asked for the fashion style of the day, only to be told: 'Lad, I'll tell you how you're going to have it cut. Off!'

'Nay, Sid', pleaded the lad.

But Sid was in no mood for arguing, and before the lad could make any further comment he added, 'Look lad, keep your cap on if you want, but, if you do, all under your cap is yours and what's outside it is mine.'

So the young man got the 'basin treatment'.

One day at the pit, Sid's transfer point became blocked by lumps of coal, and, as the coal piled up, one lump larger than the rest rolled off the conveyor and fell onto Sid's leg, trapping him against the side of a material supply tram. The hospital diagnosed a broken tibia of the right leg and, after a couple of days in the care of the medical staff, he was allowed home, although one leg was now encased in plaster.

The Saturday hair surgery, however, continued with 'business as usual', even though Sid was far from being his usual mobile self.

In order to overcome his mobility problem, it was the customer that had to move rather than the barber. First one side of the head would be trimmed to Sid's satisfaction and then the customer would simply turn his chair around so that the other side of his head could receive the same treatment.

If there was more than one customer, they they would all get one side cut and then queue up again in order to complete the hairut. This system worked very well, and as long as those who were waiting had nowhere to go, they were all quite content.

One warm Saturday afternoon, Sid set up shop in the garden, and on this occasion his customers were rather more numerous than usual. They queued patiently and contentedly in the sun while each in turn sat for the barber's trim. Each one had the right hand side of his head cut to a bristle, and Sid just managed to finish the last customer when a female voice from inside the house reminded him that it was four-thirty and that his tea was ready. 'Sorry lads', apologised Sid, 'I'll have to go in for me tea now', and added, 'Come back about six o'clock and I'll finish you off.'.

Protests from his clientele were ignored. In point of fact, they were careful not to complain too strongly, because if they did he just might not finish them off at all, and they couldn't go to another barber with half a head of hair, even if they could find a barber's shop open. Also, what about that evening in the local? With hair short and bristly on one side and rather long and unkempt on the other, they would become the butt of everyone's jokes. Sunday had to be endured as well, for Sid didn't cut hair on Sundays. No, there was not a right lot that could be said, and they all meekly rose and trooped away from the house and down the street. The kids playing around the lamp posts shouted abuse and ran off before retribution could be meted out.

Everyone returned at the appointed time and Sid completed his work, making both sides equal.

'When's t' pot coming off?' voiced one, referring to the plaster cast around Sid's leg.

'Another couple of weeks yet', he replied.

'I'll come back when you're back at work', said another as he dutifully paid his money. 'My kids laughed at me all over tea time—even our dog barked as if he didn't know me', he added ruefully.

At least the pubs were open now, and they could forget the incident and reminisce about earlier and better days over a pint of beer.

The Gas Test

E VERY colliery deputy, because of the supervisory nature of his work,
must be a competent miner with at least five years' underground
experience, of which at least two must have been spent working at the
coal face. His duties include looking after the safety of the men who are
under his charge and the making of regular inspections of that part of the
mine that has been designated as his 'district' by the Manager of the mine.

There are many important facets included in the routine inspection of
a deputy's district, by no means the least of which is the regular test for
the explosive gas normally found in coal mines, methane, or to give it its
more common name, 'firedamp'.

Firedamp is lighter than air, and, because of this feature, the gas may usually be found at or near the roof of the workings, and its presence in the mine can be detected by the use of a flame safety lamp.

Even in these modern, electronic times, the flame lamp is still used for gas detection and, indeed, is still required for such purposes by mining law. It is really an updated version of the one invented by Sir Humphrey Davy, and the detection of firedamp is possible because of the fact that, provided that the flame of the lamp is lowered so that almost all the yellow in the flame has disappeared, any gas present in the air in and around the lamp will be seen burning on the lowered flame as a pale blue nimbus of light. This feature is known as a gas cap.

The size of the gas cap depends upon the amount of firedamp present in the air, and it is very important that the deputy who is making the inspection for gas in the mine air should be able to identify the exact percentage of firedamp present at any one time, and be as accurate as possible.

The smaller percentages are the ones most difficult to see, one and one quarter per cent being the lowest amount that can normally be detected by this method, with the gas caps increasing in appearance as bigger and bigger triangular-shaped blue flames, up to about five per cent when, at about half a per cent higher, the gas and air mixture becomes unstable and explodes harmlessly in the lamp.

Mining law requires that a deputy who is in charge of a district must demonstrate his ability to identify gas caps and, if he is found to be proficient, he is given a certificate to prove that he has successfully passed the gas testing examination. This certificate must be renewed by each and every deputy at maximum intervals of five years in order to ensure that the men remain proficient.

Bill Armitage was a deputy at Renishaw Pit, where he had worked since leaving school. He was acknowledged by all to be good at his work, and also reasonably clever at picking winning horses from the lists in the daily paper, although, as he complained to one of his workmen on one occasion, 'They don't print the newspapers as clearly as they used to do when I was young.'

In fact, Bill was turned sixty and was looking forward to early retirement in a couple of years' time.

One afternoon, as Bill was crossing the pit yard at the end of the day shift, he was hailed by the training officer. 'Oh Bill, I've been trying to catch you, you're due for a gas test soon, your certificate runs out in a couple of weeks.' Sure enough, at the end of the Friday shift, Bill found a note waiting for him in the lamp room. It was from the Training Officer, telling him to report to the local Technical Institute at 9 a.m. on the next Monday morning, to take his five-yearly gas testing examination.

Monday morning arrived, as Mondays are won't to do, although for the Armitage family this particular Monday was quite different. For a start, Bill had his breakfast at the same time as his wife, and, secondly, he was able to pick his winners from the lists of runners and riders in the morning paper over a more leisurely meal than the hurried affair that he was normally accustomed to. With the aid of his good lady's reading glasses, Bill was able to make out a list of bets that he would drop into the Turf Accountant's letter-box on his way to the College.

Breakfast over, Bill made preparations to leave. 'I'm off now', he shouted into the kitchen, where Mrs. Armitage was washing the dirty dishes, adding, 'Oh, I'm borrowing your glasses, just in case.' And, with that, he was away. The College was thronging with students, but Bill soon found out where he was to go and, finding others of his ilk on similar quest, eventually presented himself in the right room.

Altogether there were eighteen pit deputies gathered for re-examination, and Bill was soon chatting away to those men that he knew from neighbouring mines. 'It's my last time', he said, adding, 'I'll be retired by the time the next five-year exam. comes round.'

One by one, the examinees were ushered into a darkened room. Here they waited in total darkness until their eyes had become accustomed to pit conditions. After about ten to fifteen minutes, again one at a time, they were taken before the examiner.

Bill's turn in the darkened room, on his own, came almost before he was ready for it and, while he waited for what seemed to be an eternity, he began for the first time to think seriously about the test that he was about to undergo. He hadn't really seen any gas caps recently. After all, Renishaw Pit was always considered to be gas-free, so there was no chance of any actual practice at the mine. Then he thought about his eyesight and fumbled in his pocket for the unfamiliar shape of the spectacle case which held his wife's glasses. Half opened, the case and contents fell with a clatter onto the floor. Bill got on to his knees and eventually, after much careful searching, managed to locate the glasses and, a little while later, the case as well.

'William Armitage.' The seemingly disembodied voice of the examiner intoned his name from the next room. Bill found the connecting door and walked in.

'You're William Armitage?', queried the examiner.

'That's right', Bill replied, adding, 'This is my last test. I'll be retiring shortly.'

The other man was silent for a while and then asked, 'Do you wear glasses?' 'No', Bill replied, 'But I've brought my wife's.' He fumbled with the case again, but his attempts to fix the spectacles on his face were pre-empted by the examiner.

'What's your wife going to do all day without glasses when you are down the pit?', he said.

Bill didn't know what to say, except, 'She won't let me take them to the pit, Mister.'

14

'Then', said the examiner, 'You had better put them back in your pocket, hadn't you?'

Bill complied with the request, and wondered just how he was going to see the tiny blue flames without optical assistance.

The examiner led Bill by the arm towards a row of flame lamps conveniently hung at eye level, and began to explain: 'Get your head below the level of the flame and, when you're ready, tell me what percentage of gas you can see on this lamp.'

Bill contemplated the blurred image before him. 'I think there's some gas on that one.', he said.

'That's the one with no gas on at all.', said the examiner flatly, adding, 'Come and look at the next one.'

It was hard work for Bill to see the small gas caps that were displayed before him, and the one and a quarter percent cap, as well as the two and the two and a half percent caps, were misidentified.

Finally the examiner led him to the last lamp in the range. On this was a comparatively large cap, one of three and a half percent. Bill was ecstatic. This one he could see! He excitedly pointed it out to the examiner and said, 'Why don't you make them all like this one, then we should be able to see them a lot easier!'

The examiner again refrained from comment, but simply pointed out to the dejected William that he had in fact failed to identify any of the gas caps and therefore had failed the test.

Poor Bill. The next day he was back at the pit, trying to explain away his failure, but he also went to the Opticians and, as soon as he got his glasses, he was back at the College for a re-test, when he passed with flying colours.

CHAPTER 6

Nugget

VIRTUALLY no horses are employed below ground in British mines these days, but at one time they were an important and useful means of transport for both coal and materials. All the pit ponies were well looked after and their hours of work regulated by law. They were well fed and housed in warm stables, presided over by tyrannical horse keepers, the tyranny being directed towards the pony drivers who were suspected of ill-treating their charges.

The horse keeper also had the unenviable task of destroying the unfortunate animal that had suffered an accident and was too badly injured to be treated by a veterinary surgeon. A captive bolt pistol was used, and there were special regulations in force to control its use below ground.

The dead animal was then loaded into a tub, it usually being necessary to tie the head and the back legs together in order to achieve the desired shape for loading.

Pit ponies were once used to haul full tubs of coal from the coal fact to a gathering point, where they were then hauled in trains by some form of rope haulage. With the advent of belt conveyors for the transport of coal, the horses were relegated to taking supplies into the workings, props and bars that were needed to support the roof as the coal was extracted.

Jumbo was one such beast, an old pony with a lot of experience and 'know-how'. One thing, he could count! In his hey-day he had been a coal haulier, pulling a run of five full tubs linked together, from the coal face, along the haulage roads to the gathering point, or passbye. Here the five tubs were unhitched and eight empty tubs substituted, to be hauled back into the coal getting area.

As soon as the required number of links had been coupled together, whether five full or eight empty tubs, Jumbo set off. If the driver had quietly coupled an extra tub onto the run, Jumbo would take the strain but nothing would make him move until one of the tubs was unhooked.

As advancing years had taken their toll, Jumbo was transferred to less exacting work as a supplies pony, where the pace was a bit slower and where his driver did not push him too hard.

Joe Smith had been in charge of taking supplies to the face, and had worked with Jumbo since the animal was given lighter duties, always stopping for a chat and a chew of tobacco with the back-ripping team in the tail gate of the district. It was here that a habit developed, that one day Jumbo put a stop to. The habit was the driver's. When the customary stop was made, Joe would drape his arms and body over the back of the animal, thus supporting his ample weight. This action was tolerated for some days—and here it is easy to assume that an animal thinks like a human being and that Jumbo must have got just plain fed-up, because he leaned back!

Gradually the driver was pushed further and further over, until the pony had Joe pinned against the side of the roadway and held him well and truly fast. It was only the efforts of the rippers, with tempting pieces of bread and fat from their snap, that eventually persuaded Jumbo to move.

Joe was not always quick on the uptake and hadn't learned a lot at school, but he never repeated his trick with Jumbo.

One day, Jumbo was being rested and Joe was told to take another horse instead, so he selected one from the stalls in the stables, noting the name of the animal from the wooden board that was hung up close by. The name was scrawled on the board in chalk, and the driver was content just to give it a glance as he led the pony out and eventually started on the first run of the day towards the face with two supplies-trams containing roof supports for the back-ripping team. Joe stopped at a convenient point, and one of the back rippers came to help with the unloading.

'Got a new pony today, Joe?', he asked, 'What's his name then?' 'Nugget', said Joe.

By now the other two members of the team had stopped work and came for a chat and a look at Joe's new charge.

'Come on, Nugget', said one, 'Have a carrot.'

The pony fed readily on the handouts that were offered to him, and then it was back to work for all of them.

Joe completed his work for the day and returned the pony to his stall. Here he removed the draw-gear, harness and blinkers, and was just about to tether the horse when the irate voice of the horse-keeper bellowed at him.

'What did you take him out for?', he yelled. 'Can't you read?', he added. 'See that notice? 'Not to go out', it says. What did you take him for? He's done two shifts now.'

The horse-keeper was obviously upset, but Joe was unmoved. 'Not to go out?', he said, 'I thought it was his name that you'd written on that board. I thought he was called Nugget.', he added.

At least he would have Jumbo back tomorrow!

CHAPTER 7

Safety Checks

THE law regulating the working of coal mines requires that the manager of the pit instigates a satisfactory system which will record exactly who is below ground at any one time. Most systems employ a checking method where brass discs or checks are collected and handed in at various times and places.

Berwyn Mine was no exception to this general rule, and the system here was organised so that when the workmen collected their pit lamps from the lamproom at the start of their shift they also took with them two brass checks that were stamped with their individual number. One of the checks was handed in to the banksman as the men entered the cage at the top of the shaft at the start of the shift. This proved that they were underground.

As the miners returned to the surface at the end of their shift, the remaining check was handed in to the deployment centre which was next to the lamproom, where also they left their lamps. This proved that they had in fact returned to the surface.

More sophisticated methods are employed at other mines, but they all serve the same purpose of ensuring that everyone who is below ground is accounted for and can be identified by his check number.

Hugh Jones was a deputy at Berwyn Pit. He was generally disliked by the men who had to work under his supervision, and also by his colleagues and by the senior management grades as well. This dislike developed, in the case of two of the coal face workmen who worked in Jones's district, to the point of hatred.

Hugh Jones' manner was always sarcastic, his scathing tongue criticised everything that the two men did, and his language was so foul that it upset even the most hardened miners. Jones openly stated that none of his men ever knew their fathers and that their mothers were never married.

One day, sometime around tea time, long after the day shift had come out of the mine, bathed and had gone home, Megan Jones, Jones' long-suffering wife, came to the pit. Hugh Jones had not come home for his tea, and, maybe surprisingly, she was concerned.

Apparently Jones' home life did not vary a great deal from his pit life, and Megan was having a hard time of it. Yet here she was, at the mine to see if he was alright.

A quick check was made to see if his lamp had been handed in. It was there in its place, as were the brass checks with his number on them. Yes, Hugh Jones was definitely out of the mine.

Megan Jones returned home and waited. By the time the pubs had shut that night, Hugh Jones still hadn't put in an appearance, and Megan put on a coat and walked round to the Police Station in the village.

'He'll be sleeping a skinful off', said the Station Sergeant, 'You know what he's like.' Having accommodated Jones in the cells on many occasions for similar reasons, the Sergeant thought very little of the matter.

Next morning, Hugh Jones did not report for work. His lamp and checks remained in their place, and another deputy was deployed to Jones' district. Everyone at the pit thought the same as the Police Sergeant—'Hugh Jones had a skinful again.'.

However, Jones was not at home and his wife again went to the Police to report that he was missing from home and work. The Sergeant said that he was busy, but he would inform the C.I.D. and the Missing Persons Branch.

Eventually, next day, a C.I.D. man toured the local public houses, asking if Jones had been seen in any of them lately. Everyone knew of Jones' capacity for ale, and also that he had not been in for the last two days.

All enquiries drew a blank, and thoughts were expressed that the man had just left home and disappeared into the wide blue yonder.

The Colliery Manager, however, had other ideas.

On the Saturday afternoon following Jones' disappearance, a dark blue van was driven into the pit yard. It pulled up by the Manager's Office. Four men descended and, together with the Manager, they went first into the pit head baths and then to the lamp room. Suitably attired and equipped for a trip below ground, they returned to the van. The rear doors were opened and two large Alsatian dogs bounded out. They were put on leads, and then the entire party quickly walked to the pit head and were wound to the pit bottom.

Here they were met by the Under Manager, a deputy and two workmen, and were led on the three-mile walk into Jones' district.

When there, a systematic search and examination of every part of the district was made. One of the C.I.D. men, for this is what the four visitors were, held a piece of cloth to the noses of the dogs and the animals then sniffed and snuffled along the dusty roads around the unit.

After an hour, the search had been narrowed down to where the two previously-mentioned coal-face workmen spent their working time. Here everything was in order, the work was tidy and was well done.

The two dogs, however, were very interested in the pack wall, about nine feet away from the face line. They moved around excitedly and began to scratch at the stones that made up the pack. The dogs were pulled away and the two workmen in the group set to work.

Carefully and slowly, the pack wall was dismantled, a difficult and dangerous operation because of the settlement of the roof. Temporary props were set as the hole was enlarged and until the object of the whole exercise came in view. First a boot and then the gruesome remains of Hugh Jones were exposed. The two colliers were arrested that night and eventually, after a short trial and the passing of three clear Sundays, they paid the extreme penalty.

CHAPTER 8

Bevin's Boys

D URING the conflict that has become known as the Second World War, the 1939 to 1945 war with Germany and Japan, many men were conscripted into British mines under a law that was passed to ensure that the industrial muscle of the country and the coal output from the pits did not suffer, so sustaining the war effort to as high a degree as possible.

The Government Minister responsible for implementing this piece of legislation was Ernest Bevin, so the conscripts became known as 'Bevin Boys'.

Quite a few of these men stayed on in the mines after the cessation of hostilities to make a career in mining, some becoming colliery officials, but most of them left the industry as soon as it was possible at the end of their service. Many men came from homes and areas of the country where there was no mining influence, and the change in their lifestyle was in many cases traumatic, to say the least.

One item of equipment, not usually discussed in polite circles, and absent from many of our pits, is toilet facilities. These most necessary adjuncts to human life may be found in factories and, although they are required to be provided for use below ground, by law, in British mines, they are a bit like bow legs, few and far between.

In some cases the necessary equipment has been made available by the management, but it has been vandalised to such an extent that it has been rendered unusable. Full receptacles also have to be emptied, work that, understandably, no-one really wanted to do, therefore, in many cases, those that were provided, when full, were left in that condition.

Although the law of the mines has, with regard to toilet facilities, been ignored, the law of nature cannot be treated in similar fashion, and when one has to go, one has to go!

In many of our towns we can see notices that say, 'Dogs must not foul the footpath.' What a pity that the animals were not taught to read!

A similar law applies on the roads below ground in the mine, not to dogs, of course, but to the miners, and although there are no prohibition signs exhibited, there are usually many signs of the law's contravention that may be discovered without too much scrutiny.

Tom Hargreaves was conscript, a Bevin Boy. He was just eighteen, and had expected to be called up for military service but his 'call up papers' had indicated that he had been drafted into the mines. So, from a well-known Public School somewhere in the Midlands, he was thrown into the deep end, as it were, and with very little introduction began his mining career at the coal face.

Tom was under the supervision of a seasoned collier, Arthur Moss. It was his duty to educate Tom in the science and art of mining coal in a safe manner, but the boy's life up to his forced employment below ground had in no way prepared him for the hard physical toil of a face worker, and it was quite some time before Tom was able to pull his weight in the combined effort of getting coal and loading it into tubs.

The coal at this particular face was got down from the solid seam by hand pick and this was Arthur's job, chipping and cutting relentlessly away at the lower section of the seam, until, with a little help from a few hefty blows of the pick, the top section would hopefully fall on its own. Tom's work consisted of shovelling the coal got down by Arthur into tubs, each holding about twelve hundredweight when full, and then pushing them by hand along the low roadways, to a gathering point where they, and tubs from other working places, were made up into long trains and were hauled to the pit bottom.

Part way through one shift, Arthur could see that Tom was not performing as well as he usually did and enquired solicitously, 'Are you alright, Tom, is anything up?'

'Well', stuttered Tom, 'I-I--I've got stomach ache, Arthur, I-I-I'll have to go-----'. His voice trailed off into silence as he looked around helplessly, for as far as he could see there was nowhere to go!

'Oh, go up the gate a bit', said Arthur rather impatiently, for the shift time was passing quickly and there hadn't been much coal mined up to the present. Tom went!

In a short while, Arthur heard his plaintive voice, 'Arthur', Tom said, 'I've been, but there's no paper.'

Arthur was on the point of losing his temper, and picked up a piece of shale from the floor and threw it towards Tom. 'Here', he said, 'Use this.'

Eventually Tom returned to the coal face, obviously relieved in more senses than one.

'You're alright now?', queried Arthur, once more bending to the task of hewing coal.

'Yes, I'm O.K. now', replied Tom as he started to shovel the loose coal into a tub, adding, 'I've put the scraper back in your coat pocket.'

Even in these so-called liberated days, Arthur's reply remains unprintable.

CHAPTER 9

Arkwright's Folly

TOM Arkwright was the colliery mechanical engineer at Frenton colliery. He had spent all his working life at the mine, starting when he left school as a fourteen-year-old boy in the fitting shop on the surface, and working his way 'up the ladder', first to become a skilled fitter and then foreman. Eventually, after forty years at the same pit, the Manager thought it fit to appoint him to his present position.

Arkwright was unqualified academically, and had earned his successive rises up the ladder simply because of his practical experience, in which he was well qualified. There were quite a few men at Frenton who were well qualified both practically and academically who had been passed over when Arkwright had been appointed, and this problem was highlighted with the advent of more modern machinery, when the engineer usually let his assistants iron out all the problems for him.

One of the assistants, Alan Barton, was detailed by Arkwright to construct a lobster-backed chute, a complicated series of bolted or welded box sections which would be used to transfer moving coal from one conveyor to another, negotiating a right angle in the process.

The chute derives its name from the similar appearance that it has to the marine crustacean, with its seemingly sectional structure.

The design of the chute is critical, so that coal flow around the bend is uninterrupted and that no blockages occur. The change in direction must be gradual, and each succeeding section is fitted at an angle to the last and is tilted downwards to allow the coal to flow smoothly.

The first problem arose when Arkwright had insisted that it was a 'left angle' and not a right angle, simply because a left-hand bend had to be negotiated. Barton had tried to explain, but Tom Arkwright had more experience and knew better.

Barton had taken a great deal of interest in the design of the chute and had carefully drawn it out to scale in order to ensure its success. On the shop floor, the necessary propping devices were prepared so that the finished article could be erected and bolted together.

Piece by piece the chute was assembled, the pride and joy of Alan Barton and his team of fitters. It was at the final moment of triumph, just as the last piece was fastened into place, that the second problem arose.

Tom Arkwright appeared in the doorway of the fitting shop.

'That's not right', he grunted roughly, 'It should be a flat curve, not like that thing you've made.'

Barton tried to explain.

'If we had built it flat', he said, 'Coal wouldn't slide down it.'

Arkwright, as usual, knew better. After all, he had forty years of experience, unlike that of his young upstart of an assistant, and he was very ready to inform all within earshot of the incompetence of Barton and his men.

Under Arkwright's direction, the whole contraption was inched out of the fitting shop and into the pit yard. Here a massive bonfire was built around it, timber piled up to the heavens, and, with a few gallons of paraffin to help it along, the pyre was ignited.

'When it gets red hot', said Arkwright, 'Squash it flat with the bucket of that bulldozer.'

After a short while, the mass of steel was white hot, and it was almost impossible to get anywhere near it. The heat radiated from the structure, which glowed like a new sun, pulsating outwards on all sides.

Eventually, when all the timber had been consumed, the heat reduced somewhat, and, with the mass approachable, Arkwright directed the bulldozer into action.

'Push the thing flat with the bucket', he shouted.

The driver complied, and the chute fell to pieces with a resounding crash.

Arkwright slunk away, to the laughter of the large number of surface workmen who had gathered to watch the spectacle.

The exercise had one good outcome, however, for, two or three days after the blaze, the pit top lads brought raw potatoes for their snap. These they roasted in the seemingly ever-glowing embers of Arkwright's Folly.

CHAPTER 10

The Great Breakthrough

FULTON colliery was being reorganised and linked up with three neighbouring pits, so that all the coal produced from the three mines could be brought along the new connecting tunnel to the Fulton colliery shafts. It would be from here that the entire output from all the pits would be wound up one shaft to the surface.

The connecting tunnel was being driven from either end, and should join up somewhere in the middle. The men from Fulton had worked at the task for some months now, and the eventual link-up was expected to take place very soon, although, at the other end, the men from the other collier, Oaklea, only worked their end of the drivage on two shifts, whereas the Fulton teams were working on a three-shift system.

Accurate surveys had been carried out, and the direction of both ends of the tunnel had been controlled by the use of laser beams. Latest checks by the surveyors had indicated that both drivages were bang on target.

Work at either end was carried out in a similar manner. First of all, holes had to be drilled into the solid rock wall that was the face of the drivage, so that explosives could then be packed into the holes to blast down the rock. About forty-five holes were needed, each one six feet deep, drilled to a pattern known as the 'burn cut'. After each round of shotholes had been fired by the shotfirer, the tunnels were advanced towards each other by about six feet.

The drilling was carried out by the face workers using compressed air operated boring machines. Firstly, a drill rod about two feet in length was attached to the borer, and each hole was bored to this depth. Then the short drill rod was exchanged for one six feet long, and the hole was then drilled to its full depth. When all the holes had been completed, the rock face was blown down, then the shattered rock was loaded out onto a conveyor to go out of the mine. When the newly exposed sides of the tunnel had been supported, the whole cycle of events could start again and another set of holes drilled into the rock face. With continual repetition of this series of events, it is easy to imagine that the two drivages were slowly and inexorably coming closer together, and soon, very soon, the two would be linked and the breakthrough would be achieved. Supervision of the workmen at the Fulton end was provided by a deputy on each shift, whose duties also included the making of safety inspections and ensuring that work continued as smoothly as possible. Overall control was exercised by the Under Manager, Bob Garten, and he paid regular visits to the Fulton tunnel on the day shift.

The work had been on the go now for about eighteen months, with hardly any stoppages and with very little trouble from the strata. The men were on good bonus payments, and were prepared to work hard and regularly. As well as being on target from a directional point of view, the planned time for the job was also being maintained, and both ends of the tunnel were probably in advance of their schedules.

From the Fulton end, faint sounds of activity could be heard from the approaching Oaklea colliery tunnel, and, when shots were being fired at either side, the sound and the shock wave could be felt in the other. It was obvious that some control would soon be required so that one of the blasts did not suddenly break through without warning into the opposing tunnel, where it was likely to cause injuries to the workmen, or even detonate prepared explosives sympathetically.

The Under Manager's visit to the Fulton tunnel face on this particular day was to assess progress and to discuss drilling and blasting times with the deputy, so that some liaison could be made with Oaklea colliery to ensure that the blasting times at the two ends of the drivage were not the same, and also to make sure that all the work was done as safely as was possible.

Bob Garten was in deep conversation with the deputy some twenty yards away from the face of the tunnel where the day shift had almost completed the work of drilling the holes into the rock face, when a shout from one of the workmen brought the two officials back to reality.

'Ay-up, Mr. Garten, ay-up, come quick, they've broken through from Oaklea, come quick!'

Garten and the deputy hurried down to the face of the tunnel, where the drilling team were standing round in an excited group. Out of the solid rock wall there protruded a drill rod with a drilling bit at the end of it.

The Under Manager was galvanised into action. He bent down near to the drill rod, cupped his hands and shouted as loud as he could. 'Ay-up, Oaklea, ay-up, you've broken through!'

Receiving no reply, Garten tried again. 'Oaklea', he shouted, 'You've broken through, don't fire, don't fire, I've got six men here, don't fire!'

Again there was no response and, with a feeling of desparation and panic, Garten took hold of the drill rod. The drilling bit was still warm from the drilling work that had just been carried out, but, to his dumbfounded amazement, the rod was easily extracted from the hole. He turned round, the shorter of the drill rods in his hand.

The drillers and the deputy were convulsed with laughter at the look of disbelief on the Under Manager's face, for it was now obvious that a hoax had taken place by simply putting the short drill rod the wrong way into a partly-bored hole.

Garten was flushed with anger at being taken in so easily, and he threw the offending rod to the floor with as much venom as he could muster and stormed off along the drivage as fast as he could go, the laughter of the men still ringing in his ears.

The drilling team bent to their tasks again, but they would always remember the best confidence trick of their lives, and it would be certain that Bob Garten would not be allowed to forget it either.

CHAPTER 11

When Christmas Comes

A COLD, frosty air blew around the pit top. It was six a.m., and the day shift queued up in the bitter wind as they waited their turn to be lowered below ground for the morning's work. Lamps had been collected from the lamp room, together with individual self-rescuers, with which every underground workman is now provided, and brass identification checks.

As the men entered the air-lock around the top of the upcast shaft, they were immediately surrounded by warmer air returning from the mine workings below, and shoulders that had been hunched against the cold were once more relaxed. One brass disc, stamped with each man's personal identification number, was handed to the banksman as the cage filled up with waiting miners, and seconds later they were engulfed in blackness as the descending cage whisked them safely but swiftly to the pit bottom. Here the men left the cage and made their way towards their working places.

Collingford colliery was one of the largest mines in the country, and had been raising a million tons of coal a year for the power station market for quite a few years. Recently there had been talk of increasing production to one and a half and maybe two million tons in future years. It was a high production mine, with all the coal faces employing high technology equipment to get the coal and load it onto mechanically driven conveyors on the face line. The roof was supported by the latest self-advancing, hydraulically-powered supports.

Most of the coal was won from the Brereton seam, ten feet thick, having a weak shale roof and a fairly soft floor. It was always considered to be a gassy seam, and, as the production of coal from the mine increased, so the amount of inflammable gas that was given off from the mined coal also became greater. To combat the extra gas emission, large volumes of fresh air were constantly circulated by the ventilating fan on the surface to dilute and remove the dangerous and unwanted methane, the very explosive gas, from the workings. Collingford was a well-managed mine with a good safety record, and relations between the management and the workforce were of the highest character, each side respecting the other. It was as ideal a mine to work at as could be possible, and the financial rewards were benefitting both the industry and the men.

Back in the mine, the men had left the shaft and walked along the tunnel set aside for them to travel on in safety to the haulage road where the locomotive was waiting. Clambering into the carriages, they settled down for the journey towards the coal faces, and two miles from the shaft bottom the train stopped for the men who worked on 49's unit to get off. It was the last day before the Christmas break, and there was a full turn-up.

The deputy checked each man against the names in his note book, and then directed each of them to their individual tasks.

Most of the coal faces in the Brereton seam were worked by a mining method known as advancing faces, where the face line, shift by shift and day by day, was driven further and further away from the pit bottom and towards the boundary of the workings. Christmasses had come and gone at Collingford pit, and evidence of Christmasses past could be seen in many parts of the mine. A shrivelled balloon here and a piece of tarnished tinsel there marked the places where Christmas had been celebrated. Twelfth Night, however, was largely forgotten, and the decorations that had temporarily brightened up the lives of the miners had been left to gather dust.

Forty-nines' Unit was a retreat face, and this meant that the method of working the face line was the opposite of the more usual advancing system and, as the coal was worked by the machines taking off strip after strip, the coal face gradually approached nearer and nearer to the shaft bottom and away from the boundary line of the workings.

At this point it is necessary to remember that the Brereton seam was noted for its high gas emission, and 49's was no exception. Quantities of methane were known to accumulate at the return end of the face, particularly in the old tunnel which was gradually being left behind as the face retreated. It was also at this place that the workmen would stop to eat their snap, part way through the shift, because it was just out of the main air current and therefore a lot warmer, although the deputy had hung up a length of plastic sheet to try and direct some of the air into the area to keep it gas free.

Christmas on 49's this year was going to be the best ever, and the men had begun to plan what they would do on the last shift before the festive season during the previous week as they chatted on their journey into the workings on the locomotive train. They were going to have a real party, and, as one man said, 'We'll start Christmas with a bang.'

He wasn't to know just how true his statement was going to be!

Each man on the unit was to contribute some item to the feast, for it was going to be a day to remember, cake had been promised, also pork pie, crisps and sausage rolls, all no doubt raided from the family larder the night before. The deputy knew from past experience that it was very unlikely that much coal would be cut and loaded, and indeed the management were aware that the whole pit would in all probability grind to a halt somewhere around mid-shift, some faces not resuming production until the New Year.

In past years, the Manager had turned a blind eye to the Christmas festivities below ground, and he was in no doubt that the coal output on this last day would be very little indeed.

The 49's machine team had got off to a good start. There was no bad roof to contend with, and they had cut and loaded two strips of coal, from one end of the face to the other and back again, before snap time. Also the conveyor belts had kept running, and there were no other hold-ups to delay production.

The deputy never found out who was responsible, but someone on 49's Unit had signalled the conveyor taking the coal along the tunnel out of the mine to stop. The face conveyor also stopped automatically, and coal getting ceased. The whole unit was at a standstill.

The electrician and the fitter took the sudden stoppage as a signal also, and immediately began to lay half-round timbers across the floor in the usual snapping area, just behind the face line. The plastic sheet, previously erected by the deputy, was cut down and laid over the timbers as a table cloth. It was looking quite homely.

The machine team from the face line had made their way to the end of the face to join the party, where edible contributions from the others had already appeared on the table. The pork pie was cut up into pieces, and a cake was similarly divided. Bowls of nuts and raisins were available, and numerous packets of crisps with exotic flavours were also produced. Unfortunately the liquid refreshment wasn't up to the standard that the men usually preferred, as the regulations forbade the use of alcohol below ground, and orange juice flowed instead of wine. About halfway through the meal, a spotlight coming up the conveyor road indicated that either the deputy or maybe some more senior official was investigating the stoppage. The owner of the light eventually revealed himself to be the Under Manager. He stayed a while, having some nuts and a few crisps, and on a promise from the men that they would be back at work and producing coal again shortly, he left to go to the pit bottom.

The deputy, meanwhile, had completed the inspection of the district and came to where his men were feasting and joined them in a belated snap, trying all the while to persuade them to resume coal-getting operations—a forlorn task! Time was passing, the normal twenty minutes' snap time had dragged on and on. An hour had passed, and there was no obvious move to return to work. Protests and threats by the deputy were ignored as if he wasn't there. At last one of the supplies men got up from his seat and, from the shoulder bag in which he carried his snap tin and water bottle, he brought out a rectangular cardboard box.

'Here's a surprise for you', he said.

All eyes turned and looked as he took the lid off the box. Inside were four Christmas crackers.

Childish excitement rippled through the gathered group of men as eager hands reached out. First one cracker was pulled, the paper hat donned while everyone laughed at the silly motto.

Standing up to get a better purchase, the machine driver and his mate pulled the second one.

The Under Manager, meanwhile, had stopped at the end of the conveyor, hopefully waiting for some sign that life had returned to normal and that coal was once again flowing off 49's.

The sudden, momentary reversal of the air current took him unawares, and for an instant puzzled him. As he realised its significance he was horrified to see a cloud of swirling dust belching out of 49's tunnel and engulfing him in choking blackness.

He fumbled for his self-rescuer and put it on.

It was obvious now that there had been an explosion, and he knew that the deadly carbon monoxide would be all around him. There was no answer from the face line when he eventually found the telephone, and all he could do was to contact the surface control room to report the incident and ask for rescue services to be sent in with as much haste as possible.

Christmas that year was going to be a time of sorrow for quite a few families, but it had certainly started, as predicted, with a bang!

Glossary

1. Banksman .... A man responsible for signalling to the driver of a winding engine that it is safe to lower the cage from the surface.

2. Chocks .... Hydraulically-controlled roof supports, having four, five or six support legs, a floor beam and a roof beam. There is usually a space between the legs of the chocks to enable men to travel through.

3. Conveyor .... A means of transporting coal and stone out of the mine. It can consist of an endless belt or a double or treble chain linked by cross members or flights.

4. Drivage .... Usually a tunnel that is being driven in coal or in stone.

5. Main gate .... The tunnel-type roadway that links the main haulage routes with the coal face. It is usually the route for the fresh ventilating air current onto the face and the route out for the coal that has been mined.

6. Pack .... A wall of stone rubble that is built into the waste alongside the main and return gates to help in the control of the lowering of the roof after the extraction of the coal.

7. Return gate ..... The roadway that leads from the coal face to the main routes out of the mine. It is the usual route by which the air that has been used on the coal faces is taken out of the mine. It is often used as a travelling route for the men and the route by which supplies are taken into the workings.

8. Return end ..... The end of the coal face that is adjacent to the return gate.

9. Ripping .... The stone that has to be brought down after the coal has been mined in order to provide adequate height in the roadways.

10. Snap time .... The customary break from the routine of work so that food and drink (usually water) can be consumed, and the workmen refreshed.

11. Spillplate .... A steel plate fastened to the waste side of a chain conveyor that is used on a mechanised coal face, so that coal that is on the conveyor will not fall off into the waste and be lost.

12. Stone drift..... A drivage in stone, a tunnel, usually inclined.

13. Tail gate........ Synonymous with 'return gate'.

14. Unit............... A part of a mine, also known as a 'district', usually the responsibility of a deputy. Can also be taken to mean the colliery itself.

15. Upcast shaft.. One of the shafts by which entrance to the mine is gained. It is used to conduct the air that has been circulated around the mine back to the surface so that it can be discharged into the atmosphere.

16. Waste............. The empty space or void that is left behind when the coal seam is extracted.

BOOKS BY
JOHN N.MERRILL
& PUBLISHED BY
JNM PUBLICATIONS

DAY WALK GUIDES

PEAK DISTRICT: SHORT CIRCULAR WALKS Fifteen carefully selected walks—3 to 5 miles—starting from a car park. The walks cover the variety of the area—the gritstone edges, limestone dales, and peat moorland. All follow well defined paths; include a pub for lunch; and are suitable for all the family. 44 pages 16 maps 32 photographs   ISBN 0 907496 16 4

PEAK DISTRICT TOWN WALKS Twelve short circular walks around the principal towns and villages of the Peak District. Including Castleton, Buxton, Hathersage, Eyam,Tissington and Ashbourne. Each walk has a detailed map and extensive historical notes complete with pictures. 60 pages 12 maps 96 photographs   ISBN 0 907496 20 2

PEAK DISTRICT: LONG CIRCULAR WALKS Fifteen differing walks 12 to 18 miles long for the serious hiker. Many follow lesser used paths in the popular areas, giving a different perspective to familiar landmarks. 64 pages 16 maps 28 photographs   ISBN 0 907496 17 2

WESTERN PEAKLAND—CIRCULAR WALKS The first book to cover this remarkably attractive side of the National Park—west of Buxton. The guide combines both long and short walks. 25 -3 to 11 mile long walks with extremely detailed maps to help you explore the area. 48 pages 23 maps 22 photographs   ISBN 0 907496 15 6

12 SHORT CIRCULAR WALKS AROUND MATLOCK 12 walks of about 4 miles long into the Matlock area rich in history and folklore and make ideal family outings. Included is an 'alpine' walk, using Matlock Bath's cable car as part of the route. 52 pages 44 photographs 12 maps   ISBN 0 907496 25 3

SHORT CIRCULAR WALKS IN THE DUKERIES More than 25 walks in the Nottinghamshire/Sherwood Forest area, past many of the historic buildings that make up the Dukeries area.   ISBN 0 907496 29 6

DERBYSHIRE AND THE PEAK DISTRICT CANAL WALKS More than 20 walks both short and long along the canals in the area—Cromford, Erewash, Chesterfield, Derby, Trent, Peak Forest and Macclesfield canals.
     ISBN 0 907496 30 X

HIKE TO BE FIT: STROLLING WITH JOHN John Merrill's personal guide to walking in the countryside to keep fit and healthy. He describes what equipment to use, where to go, how to map read, use a compass and what to do about blisters! 36 pages 23 photos 2 sketches 3 charts   ISBN 0 907496 19 9

CHALLENGE WALKS

JOHN MERRILL'S PEAK DISTRICT CHALLENGE WALK A 25 mile circular walk from Bakewell, across valleys and heights involving 3,700 feet of ascent. More than 2,000 people have already completed the walk. A badge and completion certificate is available to those who complete. 32 pages 18 photographs 9 maps
     ISBN 0 907496 18 0

JOHN MERRILL'S YORKSHIRE DALES CHALLENGE WALK A 23 mile circular walk from Kettlewell in the heart of the Dales. The route combines mountain, moorlands, limestone country and dale walking with 3,600 feet of ascent. A badge and certificate is available to those who complete the route. 32 pages 16 photographs 8 maps   ISBN 0 907196 28 8

THE RIVER'S WAY A two day walk of 43 miles, down the length of the Peak District National Park. Inaugurated and created by John, the walk starts at Edale, the end of the Pennine Way, and ends at Ilam. Numerous hostels, campgrounds, B&B, and pubs lie on the route, as you follow the five main river systems of the Peak—Noe, Derwent, Wye, Dove, and Manifold. 52 pages 35 photographs 7 maps   ISBN 0 907496 08 3

PEAK DISTRICT: HIGH LEVEL ROUTE A hard 90 mile, weeks walk, around the Peak District, starting from Matlock. As the title implies the walk keeps to high ground while illustrating the dramatic landscape of the Peak District. The walk was inaugurated and created by John and is used by him for training for his major walks! 60 pages 31 photographs 13 maps   ISBN 0 907496 10 5

PEAK DISTRICT MARATHONS The first reference book to gather together all the major and classical long walks of the Peak District between 25 and 50 miles long. Many are challenge walks with badges and completion cards for those who complete. The longest walk—280 miles —inaugurated by John is around the entire Derbyshire boundary. Each walk has a general map, accommodation list, and details of what guides and maps are needed. 56 pages 20 photographs 20 maps
     ISBN 0 907496 13 X

HISTORICAL GUIDES

WINSTER—A VISITOR'S GUIDE A detailed look at a former lead mining community which still retains a Morris dancing team and annual pancake races. A two mile walk brings you to many historical buildings including the 17th century Market House. Illustrated by old photographs. 20 pages 21 photographs 1 map
ISBN 0 907496 21 0

DERBYSHIRE INNS The first book to tell the story behind more than 150 inns in the Peak District and Derbyshire area. With details of legends, murders and historical anecdotes, the book gives added pleasure or impetus to explore the pubs of the region. Profusely illustrated with 65 photographs and a brief history of brewing in Derbyshire. 68 pages 57 photographs 5 maps ISBN 0 907496 11 3

100 HALLS AND CASTLES OF THE PEAK DISTRICT AND DERBYSHIRE
A visitor's guide to the principal historical buildings of the region. Many are open to the public and the guide describes the history of the building from the Domesday Book to the present time. The book is illustrated by 120 photographs and makes an excellent souvenir gift of one of England's finest architectural areas. 120 pages 116 photographs 4 maps
ISBN 0 907496 23 7

TOURING THE PEAK DISTRICT AND DERBYSHIRE Twenty circular routes of about 50 miles for the motorist or cyclist. Each route has a set theme, such as the gritstone edges or in the steps of Mary, Queen of Scots. Deatiled maps for each route and fifty photographs make this a useful companion to the Peak District/Derbyshire area. 76 pages 45 photographs 20 maps
ISBN 0 907496 22 9

JOHN'S MARATHON WALKS

EMERALD COAST WALK The story of John's walk up the total length of the west coast of Ireland and exploration of more than fifty islands—1,600 miles. 132 pages 32 photographs 12 maps
ISBN 0 907496 02 4

TURN RIGHT AT LAND'S END In 1978 John Merrill became the first person to walk the entire coastline of Britain—6,824 miles in ten months. The book details the route, how he ascended our three major mountains and how he found a wife. Included are more than 200 photographs he took on the walk, which is also a unique guide to our coastline. 246 pages 214 photographs 10 maps
ISBN 0 907496 24 5

WITH MUSTARD ON MY BACK John has gathered together the stories of his first decade of walking—1970-1980. Here is a collection of unique walks in Britain, from a 2,000 mile walk linking the ten National Parks of England and Wales together to a 450 mile walk from Norwich to Durham.
ISBN 0 907496 27 X

TURN RIGHT AT DEATH VALLEY During the summer of 1984, John walked coast to coast across America, a distance of 4,226 miles in 177 days. Few have walked across and none have taken so difficult a route. He crossed all the main mountain ranges, climbed 14,000 foot mountains, crossed deserts in 100 degrees, walked rim to rim of the Grand Canyon in 8½ hours, and crossed the famed Death Valley. The walk is without parallel and the story is the remarkable tale of this unique adventure.
ISBN 0 907496 26 1